TRIUMPH ON EVEREST

A Photobiography of
Sir Edmund Hillary

TRIUMPH ON EVEREST

A Photobiography of
Sir Edmund Hillary

By Broughton Coburn

NATIONAL GEOGRAPHIC SOCIETY
WASHINGTON, D.C.

For Phoebe

Published by the National Geographic Society
1145 17th Street N.W.
Washington, D.C. 20036-4688

John M. Fahey, Jr., *President and Chief Executive Officer*
Gilbert M. Grosvenor, *Chairman of the Board*
Nina D. Hoffman, *Senior Vice President*
William R. Gray, *Vice President & Director of the Book Division*

Staff for this book
Nancy Laties Feresten, *Director of Children's Publishing*
Suzanne Patrick Fonda, *Editor and Project Manager*
Judy Gitenstein, *Contributing Editor*
Marianne R. Koszorus, *Art Director*
Marcia Axtmann Smith, *Designer*
Anne B. Keiser, *Illustrations Editor*
Carl Mehler, *Director of Maps*
Joe Ochlak and Gregory Ugiansky
Map research and production
Jennifer Emmett, *Associate Editor*
Meredith C. Wilcox, *Illustrations Assistant*
Jo H. Tunstall, *Editorial Assistant*
Anne Marie Houppert, *Indexer*
Lewis R. Bassford, *Production Manager*
R. Gary Colbert, *Production Director*
Vincent P. Ryan, *Manufacturing Manager*

Library of Congress Cataloging-in-Publication Data
Coburn, Broughton, 1951-
Triumph on Everest : a photobiography of Sir Edmund Hillary /
by Broughton Coburn
p. cm.
Summary: A biography of Edmund Hillary, whose love of snow, mountains,
and the outdoor life culminated in his conquering the highest peak in the world.
ISBN 0-7922-7114-9 (hc)
1. Hillary, Edmund, Sir--Juvenile literature. 2. Hillary, Edmund, Sir--Pictorial works--
Juvenile literature. 3. Mountaineers--New Zealand--Biography--Juvenile literature.
4. Mountaineering--Everest, Mount (China and Nepal)--Juvenile literature.
[1. Hillary, Edmund, Sir. 2. Mountaineers. 3. Mountaineering.
4. Everest, Mount (China and Nepal)] I. Title.

GV 199.92.H54 C62 2000
796.52'2'092--dc21
[B]   00-027009

Cover: A triumphant Edmund Hillary relaxes at Everest Base Camp, exhausted but exhilarated by his climb. *Endsheets:* Hillary photographed this view of the Rongbuk Glacier, looking west from the summit of Everest. *Half-title page:* Hillary, followed by Tenzing Norgay, trudges along Everest's southeast ridge, gasping for each breath. *Title page*: Everest crowns the Himalaya, a mountain range that straddles the border between Nepal and Tibet. *Opposite:* Hillary helps assemble the Silver Hut, a prefabricated shelter for participants in a study on the effects of high elevation on the human body.

"Finding new adventures has never been a problem in my life—the big difficulty is finding time to do them."

Foreword

I was born in the Himalayan village of Kunde, 12,500 feet high in Nepal's Khumbu region. One of my clearest memories growing up is from 1961, when I was six years old. A group of us—all barefooted children dressed in homespun Sherpa clothing—went to greet Sir Edmund Hillary in the village of Khumjung, where he had just completed building the first school for Sherpas. Though I barely knew what a school was, I was excited and eager to become one of the first students.

Since my first day of school, Hillary has been a mentor to me and many other Sherpas. Through his explorations we learned about the world.

With Sir Edmund's help I obtained scholarships to universities in New Zealand and Canada. In 1980 I became the first Sherpa to be appointed Chief Warden of Sagarmatha (Mount Everest) National Park, after obtaining a degree in parks and recreation from Lincoln University in New Zealand. Again, Hillary was there to help me and the park, providing support for our reforestation and wildlife-conservation efforts.

Sir Edmund is respected among the Sherpas for his humanitarian work. He is affectionately known in Khumbu as *Burrah Sahib:* Great Leader. The numerous schools he has built speak for themselves. He also has constructed hospitals, health clinics, bridges, and trails and has supported restoration of our monasteries.

Sir Edmund Hillary has opened the eyes of the Sherpa people and encouraged us to venture into the world to see and learn for ourselves. Without him, I would likely be herding yaks in my tiny, remote village rather than directing a conservation program for the Himalaya.

It is my hope that, after reading this excellent book, young people everywhere will be inspired to follow in the giant footsteps of Burrah Sahib.

Mingma Norbu Sherpa
Director of Conservation
Asia and Pacific
World Wildlife Fund

With hands together, Hillary returns the respectful greetings of Sherpa school children in the village of Beni. Around his neck are *kata* blessing scarves.

When Edmund Hillary was a farm boy growing up in New Zealand, he dreamed of knights and dragons and fought imaginary villains with a stick instead of a sword. He read stories of real-life heroes late at night under the covers. Who would have guessed that one day this shy boy would become a hero to others—that he would conquer the highest mountain in the world, use tractors to reach the South Pole, and be made a knight himself?

Edmund Hillary was born on July 20, 1919, in Auckland on New Zealand's North Island. Soon after, his parents moved 40 miles south of the city to Tuakau. Edmund came from a family of pioneers. Grandfather Hillary had left England in the late 1800s and had become wealthy in India before settling in New Zealand, where he lost his fortune betting on racehorses. Grandmother Hillary, who as a young woman had traveled from Ireland to New Zealand as a governess to a British family, was resourceful enough to take over and raise Edmund's father, Percival, and his three brothers and sisters. As a young boy, Edmund was enthralled by his grandmother's stories of sailing the South Pacific.

Edmund's mother, Gertrude Clark, grew up in a remote farming community north of Auckland. When her father was kicked in the head and killed by one of his horses, Gertrude was raised by her mother and her older sisters. She was hard-working, self-reliant, and loved to play the piano. Her genteel and caring ways balanced those of Edmund's father, who could be quite strict.

Percival Hillary was managing editor of the Tuakau newspaper. He was a principled man, outraged by social injustice. His strong social conscience instilled in Edmund a lifelong desire to help those less fortunate. But Percival Hillary could be quite demanding, too, granting few holidays from the family farm. He treated his children sternly, giving Edmund "a good thumping" more than once. Edmund felt that his punishments were sometimes unfair, though they helped him develop a sense of self-discipline.

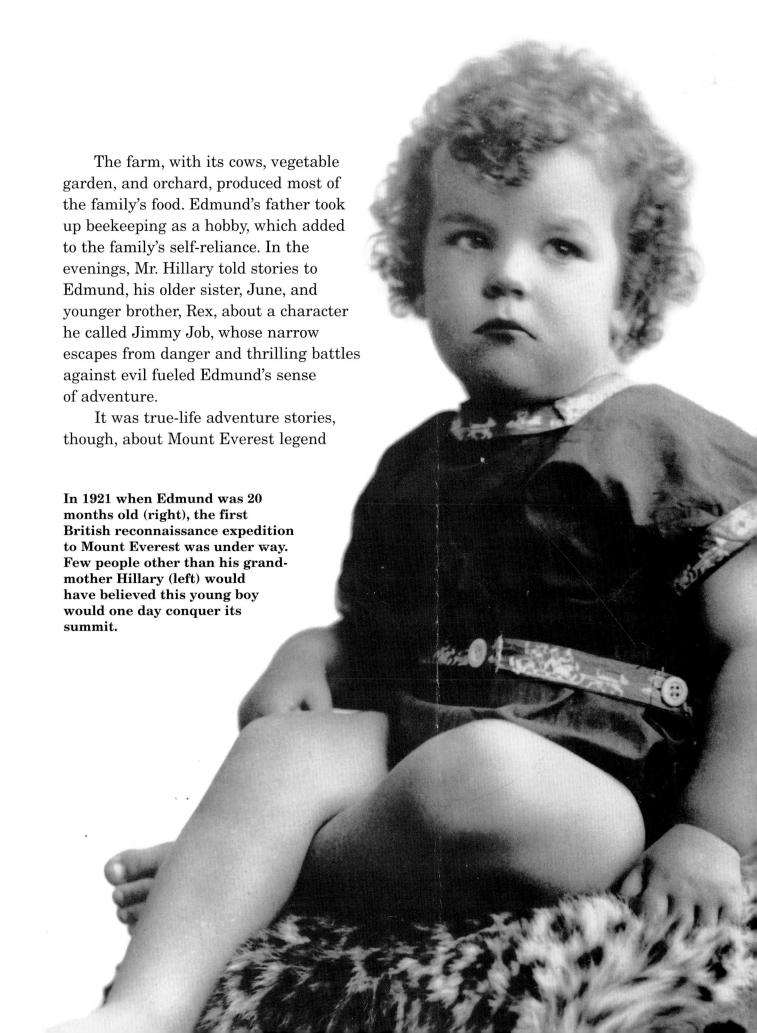

The farm, with its cows, vegetable garden, and orchard, produced most of the family's food. Edmund's father took up beekeeping as a hobby, which added to the family's self-reliance. In the evenings, Mr. Hillary told stories to Edmund, his older sister, June, and younger brother, Rex, about a character he called Jimmy Job, whose narrow escapes from danger and thrilling battles against evil fueled Edmund's sense of adventure.

It was true-life adventure stories, though, about Mount Everest legend

In 1921 when Edmund was 20 months old (right), the first British reconnaissance expedition to Mount Everest was under way. Few people other than his grand-mother Hillary (left) would have believed this young boy would one day conquer its summit.

George Leigh Mallory and Antarctic explorer Ernest Shackleton that most captured Edmund's imagination. Mallory and Shackleton never achieved their goals. Edmund dreamed of completing what they had set out to do.

Under the watchful eye of his school-teacher mother, Edmund began as an excellent student, graduating early from the primary school near his home when he was 11 instead of 13, the usual age in New Zealand. Enrolling in secondary school in Auckland two years early was a difficult thing to do, academically and socially. Edmund was gripped with fear at the new setting. He was self-conscious about the way he looked, with his scrawny physique and thin, slumping shoulders. A gym teacher took one look at him and placed him a class for physical "misfits."

At age 16, on a ten-day outing to New Zealand's Mount Ruapehu with his schoolmates, Edmund saw snow for the first time. He loved skiing and climbing the hills in the cold, brisk air. The mystery and thrill of remote, high places had captured him.

With encouragement largely from his mother, Edmund enrolled in the local university at age 16. He saved the money his father gave him for bus fare by running the five miles between the family's new home in an Auckland suburb and the school. Studies at the university became difficult and unpleasant for him, however. He retained little, failed his examinations, and felt awkward socially. After two years he returned home where, with Rex and June, he spent every spare moment tending the hives.

Hillary was 20 when World War II began. He applied to the Royal New Zealand Air Force but was told he had to wait a year before he could begin training. During this time, he traveled to New Zealand's Southern Alps and checked into a mountain lodge. One evening in the lounge, he overheard two young men telling stories about their climb to the summit of Mount Cook, the country's highest peak. Hillary was awed by their remarkable adventure—and jealous, too.

He began to schedule all his spare time around climbing, and bicycled many miles to and from the starts of his climbs.

By age 19 Ed (far right in this family portrait), with his brother, Rex, was managing the family's 1,600 bee hives. He liked the responsibility, but he shared his sister's love of hiking and longed to spend more time in the mountains.

> "I knew I had more physical energy than most, and I reveled in driving myself to the utmost."

In 1947 Hillary climbed 12,349-foot Mount Cook with his friend Harry Ayres. He considered Ayres to be New Zealand's strongest technical climber, and he learned many of his mountaineering skills and ethics from him.

Edmund finally was admitted to the air force at the height of World War II. He trained as a navigator and flew search-and-rescue missions in the South Pacific. One stopover stuck firmly in his memory. At a remote island hospital run by missionaries, he viewed with wonder the dedication, courage, and skill of a senior nurse as she tended to those who had no other access to health care. He visited the missionary school, which was educating and motivating children in a place with no history of education.

Edmund's air force career ended abruptly when a speedboat he was traveling on caught fire. He jumped overboard just before it exploded and swam to shore, but was badly burned. Dreams of climbing helped him fight the boredom of being confined to a hospital room. He healed quickly and soon after his release was ready to head for the mountains.

While climbing in the Southern Alps, he became friends with Harry Ayres and George Lowe, two of New Zealand's strongest technical climbers. Hillary was developing into a skilled and confident climber himself.

New Zealand's peaks quickly became too small for these young mountaineers. In May 1951, Hillary journeyed to northern India with George Lowe and two other friends, Earle Riddiford and Ed Cotter, where they were the first to climb 23,760-foot Mukut Parbat, in the Himalaya.

After reaching the summit, they descended to the hill town of Ranikhet, where they received a telegram that would change Hillary's life. The message was from the well-known climber and explorer Eric Shipton, a veteran of four expeditions to the north side of Mount Everest. Shipton had heard of these aggressive New Zealand climbers and was writing to ask if two of their team could join the British Reconnaissance Expedition to the south side of Everest. This approach had never been explored.

Edmund knew that this was the chance of a lifetime. Everest, the world's highest mountain, was the ultimate goal of mountaineers. The first reconnaissance to its north side had been made in 1921 by a British team approaching from Tibet. Three years and two more British expeditions later, George Mallory and Sandy Irvine were last seen very high on the mountain—heading upward through the clouds. Their disappearance left unanswered the question of whether they had reached the summit.

Edmund found ways to get in shape for the mountains in almost everything he did. He often ran from beehive to beehive, and when work was busy and the honey was "flowing," he frequently moved hives loaded with 60 pounds of honey.

"I was...learning to admire
the soundness and mature judgment that
came from wide experience."

Nepal, which stretched to the south of Everest, was completely closed to outsiders until 1950. But now its borders were open.

Hillary and Riddiford traveled to Nepal to join up with Shipton. While climbing a ridge near what is now Everest Base Camp, Hillary and Shipton spied a possible route. They would have to climb through the treacherous Khumbu Icefall, a broken, tumbling glacier littered with blocks of ice the size of entire houses. Until then the icefall had only been viewed from a distant high pass below Everest's west ridge.

On their return from the expedition, Hillary and Shipton were alarmed to hear that a team from Switzerland had been granted permission to climb Everest for both the spring and fall seasons of 1952. The Swiss would have a chance to beat the British to the top; the British would have to wait until 1953.

Hillary went home to New Zealand. He had been gone for six months, and his help was needed with the family bee business. Before leaving for Nepal, he had grown quite fond of a young woman named Louise Rose and looked forward to seeing her again. Her father was the president of the New Zealand Alpine Club and Edmund's friend. The two men spent many long hours discussing climbing techniques and routes. Louise was a music student and an excellent pianist, like Edmund's mother. More important, she shared Hillary's love for the mountains. He was delighted to discover that she was a strong climber, too.

Hillary (center) took every opportunity to climb with his close friend George Lowe (right), whose infectious team spirit and boisterous sense of humor made him an asset on the 1953 Everest expedition.

"The heroes I admired in my youth seemed to possess abilities and virtues beyond the grasp of ordinary men."

In 1951 legendary explorer and climber Eric Shipton invited Hillary to join the first British expedition to the south side of Mount Everest. While climbing, they discovered what looked like a possible route through the Khumbu Icefall. Many climbers assumed that Shipton would be chosen to lead the 1953 British Everest Expedition, and Hillary was disappointed when his role model was overlooked.

In the spring of 1952 Hillary returned to Nepal, this time to tackle some of the 20,000-foot peaks near Everest. While there, he and his climbing partners learned that Tenzing Norgay and a Swiss climber named Raymond Lambert had reached 28,000 feet before being forced back by ferocious winds and difficult conditions. The Swiss made a second attempt in the fall of that year, but high winds beat them back again. Everest was still unconquered.

Edmund Hillary and George Lowe were chosen for the 1953 expedition, but they were disappointed that their friend and mentor Eric Shipton was passed over as leader in favor of John Hunt. At Shipton's urging, they transferred their allegiances to Hunt.

En route to Nepal, Hillary arranged for a stop in Sydney, Australia. He was anxious to see Louise, who was studying music there. They spent several enjoyable days together.

In Nepal, Hillary and the other members of the expedition met Hunt and Tenzing Norgay, who had performed so well with the Swiss the year before and who had climbed high on Everest three other times. Tenzing was a Sherpa, a member of the Buddhist ethnic group whose ancestors migrated from eastern Tibet more than 400 years ago. They settled in Khumbu and Solu and in neighboring valleys to the southwest of Everest. For generations Sherpas have herded yaks and goats and carved their farms out of the hillsides.

Before climbers from the West arrived, the Sherpas had no interest in climbing the high Himalayan peaks.

In 1952 Hillary, full of confidence after a season of climbing in the Himalaya, set his sights on the ultimate prize: the 29,035-foot summit of Mount Everest (left).

"...I have had sufficient strength
and determination to meet
my challenges..."

22

To ferry supplies up Everest, climbers approaching from the south must make numerous trips through the treacherous Khumbu Icefall, with its towering ice pinnacles, gaping crevasses, and rumbling avalanches. It took Hunt's expedition more than a week to find a route through the maze.

23

> *"I felt we would give Everest all we had—but there was no certainty of success—"*

But they discovered that their skill in navigating the difficult terrain could bring much needed income to their impoverished villages, and they began to help the climbers. On Himalayan expeditions, Sherpas typically arranged transport for several tons of gear, then carried loads high on the mountain, climbing alongside their foreign team members.

Before the 1953 expedition began, Hunt's team toured Kathmandu, Nepal's exotic capital city, which, with no road access to the outside world, had few modern conveniences and only a handful of cars. Simply getting to Kathmandu had taken nearly a month of travel by plane, train, truck, and on foot. Carrying in the hundreds of loads of equipment and supplies had taken even longer. Hillary was anxious to get on the trail and into the mountains.

The three-week, 200-mile approach to Everest Base Camp served an important purpose: It allowed the teams' bodies to gradually adapt to an increasingly higher altitude, and most of the men reached camp feeling healthy and breathing comfortably.

Base Camp was slightly less than 18,000 feet above sea level. A person taken there quickly from

John Hunt (left) came from a military background and was largely unknown in climbing circles before being chosen to lead the 1953 British Everest Expedition. At right, Hillary listens as George Lowe talks with Base Camp using a two-way radio.

sea level—by helicopter, for example—would likely die within a day or two from high-altitude sickness. Taken from sea level directly to the summit of Everest, a human would not survive for more than an hour! A gradual ascent gives a person's body time to adjust to the lower atmospheric pressure and the reduced amount of oxygen available at higher altitudes. This process is known as acclimatization. A climber who is acclimatizing first begins to breathe more deeply to draw more oxygen into the lungs. Over a period of weeks the body produces more hemoglobin, the protein that cells use to carry oxygen to muscles and organs. The increased hemoglobin transfers oxygen to the organs more efficiently.

Several days before reaching Base Camp, the Everest expedition made an important stop at the Tengboche Monastery. The Sherpas and their British and New Zealand companions made offerings to the Tengboche Lama, the high Buddhist priest of the region. In return, they received blessings from him for their safety and success. He also warned them to look out for the yeti, or Abominable Snowman, which he claimed had once invaded the monastery grounds.

The expedition's first task was to find a safe route through the dangerous Khumbu Icefall. To transport equipment and supplies to camps higher on the mountain, the team had to make several trips through the icefall and then descend to Base Camp to rest and regain lost weight.

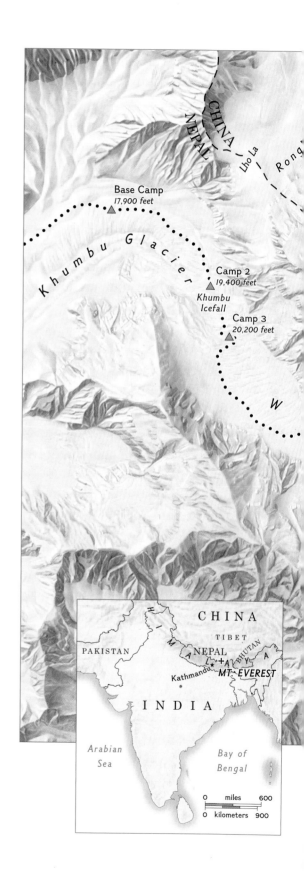

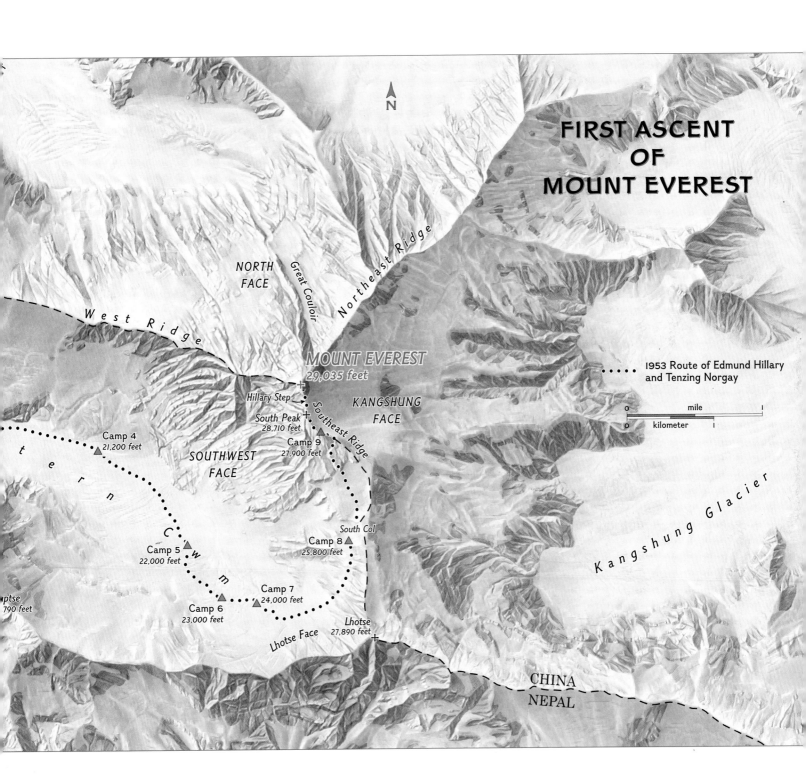

FIRST ASCENT OF MOUNT EVEREST

N

NORTH
FACE

Great Couloir

Northeast Ridge

West Ridge

MOUNT EVEREST
29,035 feet

Hillary Step

South Peak
28,710 feet

KANGSHUNG
FACE

Southeast Ridge

Camp 9
27,900 feet

Camp 4
21,200 feet

SOUTHWEST
FACE

South Col

Camp 8
25,800 feet

tern

C

w

m

Camp 5
22,000 feet

Camp 7
24,000 feet

ptse
790 feet

Camp 6
23,000 feet

Lhotse Face

Lhotse
27,890 feet

Kangshung Glacier

CHINA
NEPAL

•••• 1953 Route of Edmund Hillary
and Tenzing Norgay

0   mile   1

0   kilometer   1

**Unconquered until 1953, Everest now has been climbed by more than 1,000 people.
At least 150 have lost their lives attempting to reach the summit.**

"In a sense, fear became a friend—"

Hillary attacked the icefall with gusto, cutting steps for the climbers' boots, wriggling through cracks in the ice, and setting up bridges across crevasses—deep fissures or cracks in the glacier. Today, climbers can kick their way directly up or down ice walls using front point crampons—sharp spikes attached to climbing boots, with prongs pointing toward the front.

Hillary was often in the lead. In many places the team had to walk beneath giant walls of ice and ice pinnacles, called seracs, that could topple over at any moment, and avalanches were a constant threat.

On one of his passages through the icefall with Tenzing, Hillary leaped across a crevasse. As he landed on the far side, the snow beneath him broke away, and he found himself falling. Tenzing, who was roped to him, thrust his ice ax into the snow as a belay, or anchor, and wrapped the rope around it. The rope became taut, and Hillary came to a stop at the other end, dangling in space as the ledge of snow he had jumped onto only moments earlier went crashing into the depths far below him.

Tenzing had saved Hillary's life. Recognizing the Sherpa's great skill and enthusiasm for climbing, Hillary began to encourage Hunt to consider the two of them as a possible summit team.

The expedition methodically worked its way up the mountain in stages, spending nearly two weeks at Camp 4 (Advance Base Camp, or ABC) at 21,200 feet. From here they established higher camps, pushing on to the South Col, the high, windy pass between Everest and Lhotse. Here they set up Camp 8 at 25,800 feet. This was the beginning of the so-called Death Zone. At this altitude, a climber must attempt the summit within a day or two or retreat to safer elevations below. Remaining at that level with so little oxygen would cause increasing weakness and certain death.

On May 26, John Hunt, Charles Evans, Tom Bourdillon, and Da Namgyal Sherpa set out from Camp 8 to make the first attempt on the summit.

Teamwork is essential to the success of any expedition. Here a Sherpa stands ready to stop the fall of his partner if the wall of the crevasse collapses.

> ## *"I was frequently scared and often tired but there were few moments I would have willingly missed."*

As planned, Hunt and Da Namgyal carried supplies to 27,350 feet then returned to the South Col, exhausted. Evans and Bourdillon reached 28,700 feet—higher than any person had been known to climb before. They did not have enough oxygen to go on and still make a safe descent. Reluctantly, they returned to Camp 8. Charles Evans reported to Hillary that the summit ridge didn't appear to be climbable. Undaunted, Hillary was eager to find out for himself.

Hillary and Tenzing, along with the support team of George Lowe, Alf Gregory, and Ang Nyima Sherpa, slowed by the altitude and their heavy packs, reached the cache of supplies left the day before at 27,350 feet. Here, they piled more oxygen tanks, sleeping bags, and a tent onto their loads. Hillary hoisted 60 pounds onto his back—a remarkable weight in that oxygen-starved atmosphere—and pushed on, struggling for every step up the mountain. At 27,900 feet, they found a narrow, sloping shelf for a tent site. Lowe, Gregory, and Ang Nyima, having finished their job, turned back to the South Col. Hillary and Tenzing were on their own.

They hoped the high winds wouldn't blow them away during the night. By Hillary's calculation, they would have enough bottled oxygen to breathe while they tried to sleep for a few hours. He hoped that would leave enough to reach the summit and return to the South Col.

Tenzing melted piles of snow on a small stove, to replenish the water their bodies had lost. At high altitudes, climbers become dehydrated, losing water mainly through their breathing. They inhale and exhale much faster and more deeply than at sea level, and each time they breathe out, moisture-laden air leaves their bodies.

At Camp 4 Hillary checks Tenzing's bottled oxygen apparatus. Designed to provide extra oxygen, the equipment was heavy and unreliable. Sunlight reflected from the snow generates intense radiant heat. For protection, Hillary wears a striped sun hat his sister made from a child's play suit.

It is difficult to sleep at an elevation of 27,900 feet, in temperatures well below zero. Tenzing described the hurricane-force winds as "the roar of a thousand tigers." The gusts seemed only to worsen their feelings of loneliness and fear.

In the morning, Hillary's boots were frozen solid. Their start was delayed an hour while he thawed his boots over the stove. With Tenzing in the lead, they set out, gaining height slowly but consistently until they ran into a vertical jumble of rock 40 feet high. It stood between them and the summit. Hillary noticed a jagged crack toward the steep Kangshung Face to the east and crawled into it. He wriggled and jammed his way to the top of this vertical wall, using every small handhold he could find. Tenzing followed. This rock feature is now known as the Hillary Step.

They pushed on, unsure how to find the summit other than simply to keep climbing upward. At 11:30 a.m. on May 29, 1953, they realized they could climb no higher. Edmund Hillary and Tenzing Norgay were standing on top of the world!

They hugged each other heartily. Hillary photographed Tenzing holding up his ice ax, on which he had tied together flags of Nepal, India, the United Nations, and the United Kingdom. He also took pictures looking out in every direction over the surrounding mountains, to prove they had made it to the summit. Hillary looked for signs that Mallory and Irvine had been there but found nothing.

They had been on top for 15 minutes. Tenzing placed the flags in the snow, along with some offerings to the goddess that the Sherpas believe resides within Chomolungma, the Tibetan name for Everest. Then they descended quickly, because their supply of bottled oxygen was running low.

To avoid falling thousands of feet off the Kangshung Face, Hillary and Tenzing again took turns cutting steps with their ice axes. Arriving at the South Col in less than four hours, they were greeted by George Lowe, carrying a mug of soup. He congratulated them heartily, saying he figured they had "knocked it off."

There was no two-way radio contact with Advance Base Camp, so Hunt and the other expedition members did not learn of their success until the

Hillary snapped this now famous photograph of Tenzing standing on top of the world. When asked why no pictures were taken of himself, he replied, "Tenzing is no photographer, and Everest was no place to begin teaching him."

THE ILLUSTRATED
LONDON NEWS

The World Copyright of all the Editorial Matter, both Illustrations and Letterpress, is Strictly Reserved in Great Britain, the British Dominions and Colonies, Europe, and the United States of America.

SATURDAY, JUNE 27, 1953.

next afternoon when the team arrived. As they approached ABC, Hillary and Tenzing were too tired to shout or signal their victory, so George Lowe waved his ice ax toward the summit. With tears in his eyes, John Hunt threw his arms around Hillary's shoulders, and everyone hugged all around. The Sherpas looked at Tenzing with deep respect and amazement, proud that one of their own had reached the top.

Relaxing at ABC, Hillary felt a sense of personal achievement, but he didn't think the world would take much notice. *London Times* correspondent James Morris, who was also at ABC, knew otherwise. He made his way down the valley to Namche Bazar, arriving in less than three days, to send a message to the British Embassy in Kathmandu. The message was delivered in code via the army radio so that the *Times* would retain its "scoop" on the story. The timing was excellent: The news of Hillary and Tenzing's triumph coincided with the June 2 coronation of Britain's monarch, Her Majesty Queen Elizabeth II.

While walking from Base Camp back to Kathmandu, a mail runner handed Hillary a letter addressed to him as "Knight of the British Empire." He and the team assumed it was a joke, but the letter confirmed that the Queen wanted to bestow knighthood on him.

Hillary found the prospect of being called "Sir Edmund" unsettling at first. He had never really approved of titles and couldn't imagine possessing one himself. Looking at his dirty pants, all he could think was, "My God! I'll have to get a new pair of overalls."

When Hillary, Tenzing, and Hunt reached Kathmandu, crowds welcomed them as heroes. Tenzing was awarded the Star of Nepal.

The *Illustrated London News* published the exclusive story of Hillary and Tenzing's conquest of Everest, bringing them worldwide attention. Hillary always felt uncomfortable that Tenzing was not knighted as he and Hunt (above) were.

"...my life has been strung together by a series of friendships...— most of all, Louise—"

The reception in the United Kingdom was equally overwhelming. Even though he was from New Zealand, the British people embraced Hillary as their own. After all, New Zealand was part of the British Empire. A garden party was hosted by the Queen and her husband, the Duke of Edinburgh, at Buckingham Palace. Then Hillary and Hunt were taken into the royal quarters, where they were asked to kneel onto a low stool. They were about to be officially knighted! The Queen said a few words and then gently tapped Hillary on each shoulder with a sword.

On his way back to New Zealand, Hillary stopped in Sydney to visit Louise. She was thrilled with his success. Louise and her parents had always known Hillary would excel. He wanted to marry Louise, but he was scheduled to leave on a worldwide lecture tour. They decided to get married right away so that Louise could accompany him abroad.

After an engagement of only nine days, they had a simple wedding on September 2, 1953, in Auckland. The bride and groom emerged from the marriage chapel beneath an arch of ice axes. They left for London the following day. On the lecture tour, Hillary was pleased to see that the press and officials were charmed by Louise's friendly, gregarious nature—the qualities that had attracted him to her in the first place. Louise helped share the burden of public appearances, which her husband found tiring.

They returned to New Zealand three months later, exhausted. They built a house and worked with the Hillary family bees, trying to balance public attention with rural family life. In the next few years, Louise gave birth to a son, Peter, and then a daughter, Sarah. Sir Edmund greatly enjoyed family life. It was another new adventure.

After Everest, Hillary wasted no time proposing to Louise Rose. They were married on her 23rd birthday in what was called in New Zealand the wedding of the year. A smiling George Lowe (in the background) served as best man.

ir Ernest Shackleton was one of Hillary's childhood heroes, and the thought of fulfilling Shackleton's goal of crossing the southernmost continent appealed to him. Hillary was asked to join the British Commonwealth Trans-Antarctic Expedition as leader of the New Zealand team. Although it was difficult to leave his young family, he knew he had to go.

Antarctica—with an ice cap almost two miles thick in places—is the coldest place on Earth, and dry winds scour its surface endlessly. Expedition leader, Vivian Fuchs, intended to begin at Shackleton Base, on the opposite side of Antarctica from Hillary's party, and travel 2,000 miles across the continent. Hillary's team was to depart from Scott Base and establish a supply depot for Fuchs 500 miles from the South Pole. Both parties were equipped with tractors specially adapted for snow travel.

For weeks Hillary's tractor caravan fought high winds, dense fog, and deep, drifting snow. The temperamental snow vehicles were nearly swallowed by countless hidden crevasses. Nowadays, Global Positioning System (GPS) devices take readings from satellites, and within seconds establish a traveler's location anywhere in the world. But in the 1950s there was no such technology. Hillary, the former air force navigator, had to calculate their positions using his sextant, a hand-held device that measures the angles of stars and celestial bodies.

Deep snow, high winds, and frigid temperatures slowed the expedition's travel across the Antarctic continent. Disaster was inches away for this tractor when the snow bridge it was crossing gave way, revealing this gaping crevasse.

"Big expeditions are rarely as much fun as small ones—"

Gale force winds battered the team for days on end. During the 20 hours of light each day, they spent most of their time shoveling snow, repairing equipment, and preparing camps.

"...when I was absent from home for long periods, Louise kept me alive in the family's thoughts..."

When cross-referenced to the accurate time, he was able to determine the team's location. The sun and stars were seldom visible, however, and Hillary was in constant fear of becoming lost.

In mid-December 1957 Hillary and his team reached the point where they were to drop supplies: Depot 700. He calculated they had enough fuel to travel the 500 additional miles to the Pole itself. So, they abandoned all non-essential gear and powered on for long hours, barely able to keep their eyes open from lack of sleep. Eighty-two days after they had departed Scott Base, and with their fuel nearly gone, they reached the South Pole. Two weeks later when Fuchs and his team arrived, Hillary and his men were flown back to Scott Base. Hillary later met Fuchs at Depot 700 and helped the expedition complete its traverse of the continent.

Throughout the expedition, Hillary missed his family terribly. He was able to speak with Louise on the radio, though this often only worsened his homesickness. When he returned to the quiet and peace of home life in New Zealand, he postponed the Antarctic expedition's lecture tour so he could spend more time with his family. Peter and Sarah were now old enough to be entranced by the Jimmy Job stories that Hillary's father had told him. In 1959, a year after Hillary's return from Antarctica, Louise gave birth to their third child, Belinda.

The Himalaya and the hospitality of the Sherpa people still held Hillary's heart, and he now hoped to find a way to get back to these mountains. Two questions continued to intrigue him: Did the yeti really inhabit the higher mountains of Sherpa country? And, now that Hillary and Tenzing had proved it was possible to climb Everest, what actually happens to the human body at such high altitudes?

Ed and Louise, with their children Peter (left), Belinda (center), and Sarah, traveled to San Francisco in 1962. They spent that summer driving through national parks in the United States and Canada.

In 1959, Hillary organized an expedition with his friend and climbing partner Peter Mulgrew to Khumbu, the heart of the Sherpas' homeland. En route, they saw unusual tracks in the snow and obtained heavy, furry skins that the Sherpas claimed were from the yeti. They photographed yeti scalps carefully locked up in monasteries and saw the eerie, bony skeleton of a yeti hand.

At 19,100 feet on the shoulder of Ama Dablam, the beautiful peak with a double hump, they set up their warmly insulated Silver Hut, to begin six months of medical studies on the human body's response to altitude. They also wanted to know how the process of acclimatization works. Does a climber's mental capacity change with altitude? Could a climber suffer permanent brain damage as a result of lack of oxygen? The data they collected added significantly to the body of science that relates to high-altitude physiology.

The team members dug and cleared a small airstrip at 15,000 feet, one of the highest landing fields in the world. The strip was designed for flying in relief supplies for Tibetan refugees who were escaping into Nepal from the Chinese occupation of Tibet, which began in 1959. Later it would be used to bring supplies for building the first Sherpa school at Khumjung.

Hillary was still anxious to solve the mystery of the yeti. He and the research team asked village elders if they could take yeti scalps and yeti skins to the United States for testing. The elders agreed, but only if a villager could accompany them. Konjo Chumbi was selected.While the Silver Hut studies were still underway, Hillary toured Europe and the United States with the Sherpa. In Chicago, tests of the skin samples proved

Thami (left) is a typical Sherpa village, located in a valley high on the south-western slopes of the Himalaya where the legendary yetis are said to roam. On occasion climbers have encountered footprints supposedly made by the yeti. But photographs have proved the tracks are either fakes, like the one above, or have been enlarged by snowmelt and actually belong to humans or some smaller animal. The 14-inch ice axe is for scale.

they were from the Himalayan blue bear and that the scalp had been fashioned from the hide of a serow, a rare member of the goat-antelope family.

In light of these findings, Hillary had to conclude that the yeti is a mythological creature. To the Sherpas, though, the menacing and boisterous yeti continues to live in the shadows of the high peaks.

Louise and June Mulgrew, Peter's wife, came to Khumbu during the spring of 1961. The trails were lined with orchids, primulas, and several varieties of tall, blooming rhododendrons. With delight, Hillary experienced Khumbu through Louise's eyes.

During this time, Hillary and Peter Mulgrew almost lost their lives attempting to climb Mount Makalu. When they reached 23,000 feet, Hillary came down with cerebral edema, a type of altitude sickness in which the brain swells, and he had to be carried partway off the mountain. Mulgrew suffered from frostbite, and eventually both his legs had to be amputated below the knee.

Sir Edmund had long appreciated all that the Sherpa people had done for him. Over the years, the Sherpas had provided him and his colleagues with so much help, guidance, and kindness that he was overcome with a desire to help them in return. He spoke with Urkien Sherpa, a leading member of several of his expeditions, to find out what he could do. "Our children have eyes, but they are blind," Urkien told him. The Sherpas were becoming aware that the world around them was changing and sensed that in order to prosper, they would need to learn about it and participate in it. Clearly, education was the key to their future.

Edmund was strongly affected by Urkien's plea. He began to raise money from sponsors and recruited a Sherpa teacher from Darjeeling, India. In 1961 the Khumjung school—Khumbu's first—was inaugurated and blessed by the Tengboche Lama, the same lama who had blessed the 1953 Everest expedition. As a result of the school's success, Hillary received petitions to build other schools in Khumbu and nearby Solu.

The sure-footed yak, a long-haired breed of cow, is widely used by the Sherpas to carry food and supplies to remote villages and to transport supplies for climbing expeditions. For centuries Sherpas have taken their yaks on trading trips across glaciers and through high mountain passes into Tibet. Sherpas say that some yaks can sense a hidden crevasse and signal its presence by pawing at the snow.

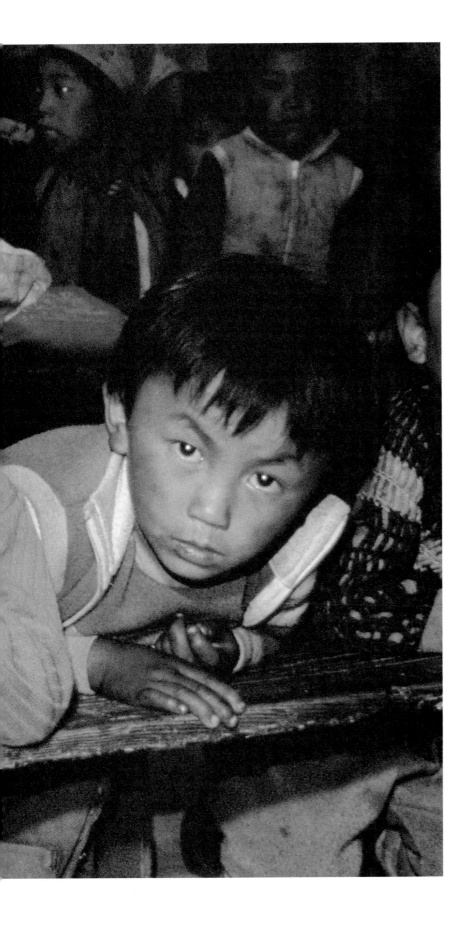

"[The Sherpas] looked after me like a favored and rather helpless child,..."

Eager to learn, these children attend the first school Hillary built in Khumjung. Without local schools, Sherpa children would remain illiterate or be sent to school in Kathmandu, where they would lose their fluency in the Sherpa language and culture. Throughout Khumbu, boys and girls attend school in roughly equal numbers.

It was rewarding to see a schoolhouse "rise up from scratch," fashioned from the rock he used to climb. There were also a growing number of requests for foot bridges, hospitals, and drinking-water systems.

At a yak pasture near Lukla, Hillary constructed a second airstrip for bringing in materials for the new construction projects. This airfield was leveled by Sherpas doing traditional line dancing, arms interlinked, singing and stamping their feet back and forth across it.

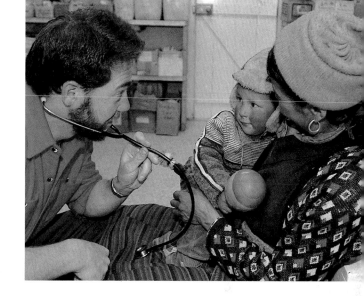

Louise shared her husband's love for the Sherpas and their mountain homeland. They both looked forward to the day when their children would be old enough to travel to the region. In 1966 Peter, Sarah, and Belinda traveled to Khumbu for the first time. The Sherpas were thrilled to have the Hillary children as guests in their houses—family to family—and spoiled them with constant attention and their tastiest food.

With the completion of the Kunde Hospital in 1966, Sherpa villagers witnessed the miracle of basic health care. Ang Duli, the wife of Hillary's close friend Mingma Tsering, had been pregnant 11 times but had given birth to only two children, both of whom were handicapped. Tests showed this was due to a shortage of the mineral iodine in her diet. After iodine treatments at the hospital, she gave birth to a healthy child, as Sherpa women now do routinely.

In 1975, the Sherpas of Solu asked Hillary to help them construct a similar hospital in Phaphlu. To oversee this work, Hillary decided to move Louise and Belinda from New Zealand to Kathmandu for a year, while Peter and Sarah attended school in India.

Hillary (left) contributed much of his own labor to projects sponsored by the Himalayan Trust, which he founded. Here he works on a school in Gumila village, one of 30 constructed to date throughout Nepal's Solukhumbu District. A Canadian doctor (above) checks a Sherpa child at the hospital in Kunde. Doctors provide high-quality medical care and educate the local people about sanitation, hygiene, and preventative health care. Only a few elderly Sherpas are still reluctant to visit a hospital, believing it is a place where people go to die.

"God knows if I'll have the courage to go on living."

While waiting in Phaphlu for a small plane carrying Louise and Belinda, Hillary learned that it had crashed after taking off from Kathmandu, killing them both.

Hillary was numb with sorrow. He and Louise had talked about death, but he had always assumed that he, as the one who took risks, would be the first to die. He wondered if he would have the courage to go on living, but he realized he had to for the rest of his family. Peter and Sarah came from India for the funeral in Kathmandu. Louise and Belinda were cremated in Nepalese fashion.

Distraught and heartbroken, Hillary soon returned to Phaphlu to work on the hospital. The Sherpas had fashioned an altar there, and each day they lit butter lamps and offered ceremonial scarves and flowers in memory of Louise and Belinda.

After the hospital was constructed, Hillary knew he had to shake off his depression and feelings of loss. Working with volunteers, his brother, Rex, and his Sherpa friends on the Himalayan projects was the only way he knew to do this, and there seemed to be no end to the tasks to be undertaken. He established the Himalayan Trust as a means of raising funds and managing the projects.

Hillary walks past a mani wall, one of many that line the trails. The walls are made of stones engraved with Tibetan Buddhist prayers. Sherpas walk around these walls in a respectful, clockwise direction.

In the late 1970s Hillary was struck again by cerebral edema while climbing with his son in the Indian Himalaya, following their jet boat expedition up the Ganges River. He realized he could no longer climb at high altitudes. Fortunately, the challenges of raising funds and helping the Sherpas were worthy alternative to his life of adventure and discovery. The timing was perfect: His fame was growing, and sponsors were offering more and more of the money needed to expand this important work.

Hillary's life had become entwined with that of the Sherpas. He lived in their homes and played with their children. He depended on them for guidance, judgment, and sheer manpower. Indeed, three decades after Hillary's ascent of Everest, the Sherpas had changed as much as Hillary had. Their living standards had improved, and many had begun to travel to Kathmandu and the world beyond.

At the same time, increasing numbers of foreign trekkers were visiting Khumbu. Hillary noticed that the Sherpas were burning more and more firewood in their trailside lodges for cooking and heating. As a result, the forests were being cut down at an alarming rate. The government of Nepal was doing little to address the problem, so Hillary and his Sherpa colleagues decided to establish tree plantations.

To protect this beautiful region, Hillary helped with the creation of Sagarmatha National Park. Since 1976 when the park was established, three Sherpas—Mingma Norbu, Lhakpa Norbu, and Nima Wangchu—have been assigned in turn as chief wardens.

Sherpas use firewood for most cooking and heating, not only for themselves but for the growing number of trekkers in the Himalaya. As a means of halting the destruction of local forests, Khumbu was designated as Sagarmatha National Park. Along with other educated Sherpas, Mingma Norbu (above), Director of Conservation for Asia and the Pacific for the World Wildlife Fund, has worked to establish tree nurseries where seedlings are grown for transplanting.

"Tenzing had substantially greater personal ambition than any other Sherpa I had met..."

In 1984 Hillary received a phone call from New Zealand's Prime Minister, David Lange, who offered him the position of New Zealand High Commissioner to India, Nepal, and Bhutan. He would be based in New Delhi, India, and would be responsible for looking after New Zealand's interests in that part of the world, overseeing development projects, and keeping his country informed of issues and events in the region.

In 1986 while serving in New Dehli as high commissioner, Sir Edmund was saddened to learn that his partner on Everest, Tenzing Norgay, had died in Darjeeling. Political tension had gripped that region of India, but Sir Edmund resolved to make the journey for Tenzing's funeral. June Mulgrew, the widow of his longtime friend Peter, accompanied him. Over the years, she had come to know Tenzing and wanted to pay her respects. As is customary among Buddhists, who believe in reincarnation, the atmosphere at the cremation was lively, not somber. The Sherpas know that Tenzing will return to see them again.

Hillary experienced one of his proudest moments in the spring of 1990. He was at home in New Zealand when he received a phone call from his son via walkie-talkie and satellite. Peter was standing on the summit of Everest! Peter told his father of the extreme difficulty he had encountered negotiating the Hillary Step and complimented him on the climbing skills that had enabled him to overcome that challenging rock wall in 1953. Ever since Peter was injured in a frightening accident on Ama Dablam that claimed the life of a teammate, Hillary has been concerned for his son's safety. But he feels that

Hillary and Tenzing, shown here relaxing at Camp 4 after their descent from Everest's summit, remained friends until the Sherpa's death in 1986. Hillary admired Tenzing as a climber and as a person. He attributed their conquest of Everest to their ability to work as a team.

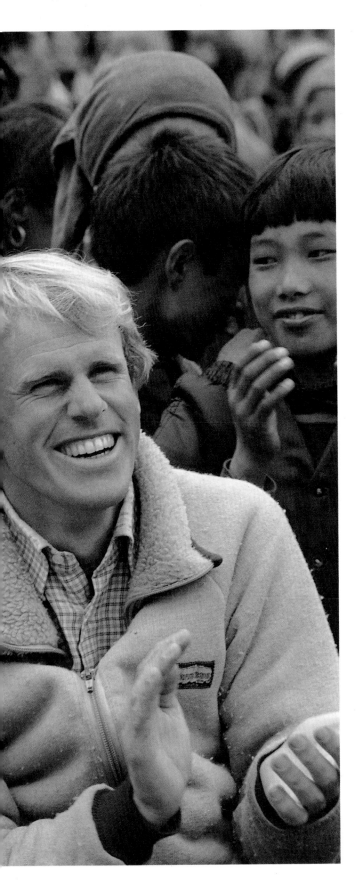

if Peter is going to take risks, those decisions must be his own, so he does not stand in his son's way.

In 1995, Queen Elizabeth bestowed on Hillary the Order of the Garter, the highest of England's knightly orders, or awards. Dressed in a cloak and feathered hat, he was joined in this ancient ceremony by Lady Thatcher, former prime minister of the United Kingdom. Looking back at his poor academic record at the university in New Zealand, Hillary finds it slightly ironic that in addition to the two titles he has received from the Queen, he has written several books, been awarded five honorary doctorates, and become a competent fundraiser and project manager.

Hillary has always considered himself a man of modest abilities whose achievements have resulted from "a goodly share of imagination and plenty of energy." Sir Edmund is a highly principled man, just as his father was. He is dedicated to helping the Sherpas withstand the changes brought to their home-land by the thousands of outsiders who have come to climb and trek in his footsteps. The media made Edmund Hillary a hero when he reached the roof of the world, but his efforts on behalf of the Sherpa people may be the true measure of his triumph on Everest.

After the deaths of Louise and Belinda, Hillary and Peter became closer. Here, in Khumjung, father and son participate in a ceremony commemorating the 30th anniversary of the conquest of Everest. Peter also has helped with bridge building and other Trust projects.

"We have been going for over thirty years now and the local people know that if we promise to do something we can be trusted to carry it out."

Afterword

Each year despite his declining health, Sir Edmund, now 80, and his wife, Lady June, whom he married in 1989, visit teacher training workshops, tree nurseries, bridges, drinking-water systems, ancient Buddhist monasteries undergoing rehabilitation, and other projects funded by the Himalayan Trust. They travel mainly by helicopter, because Hillary is no longer able to stay long at the high elevations of most Sherpa villages. At each stop the "Kindhearted Parents," as they are affectionately known, are greeted by scores of Sherpas offering *katas*—blessing scarves—and more petitions for help.

The "Hillary schools" built throughout Solukhumbu District provide second and third generation Sherpas with the knowledge and skills needed to protect their environment, participate in the local democratic process, and benefit from the business opportunities offered by mountain tourism. Although the schools are now run by the government of Nepal, the Himalayan Trust, with funding from the American Himalayan Foundation and other donors, continues to support the teachers and raise funds for maintaining and improving the buildings. Some of the labor is provided by foreign volunteers, and Hillary's brother, Rex, has provided important engineering skills. But most of the work is done by the Sherpas themselves. Hillary has always insisted that the projects rely on native techniques and materials. Ang Rita Sherpa, Chief Administrator of the Himalayan Trust in Nepal, represents the new generation of Sherpas who are beginning to guide their own development thanks to Hillary's efforts. In 1998 he was honored by the Dalai Lama, religious leader of Tibetan Buddhists, for his achievements.

Hillary has reached the top of the world. But this exceptional—and exceptionally modest—man has found something more rewarding and enduring to leave on Everest than his footprints. His legacy of caring will live on long after he is gone.

The "Kindhearted Parents," Sir Edmund and Lady June, adorned with *kata* scarves, rest along a trail in their beloved Khumbu.

Chronology

1919	Edmund Hillary is born in Auckland, New Zealand, on July 20
1936	Class trip to Mount Ruapehu, his first experience in the mountains
1939	New Zealand enters World War II
1944	Joins the air force, trains as a navigator, and is posted in the South Pacific
1945	Burned in a boat accident; World War II ends
1950	Tours Europe with his parents; climbs in the European Alps
1951	Climbs in the Himalaya as part of a New Zealand team; joins Eric Shipton on a reconnaissance expedition to Mount Everest
1952	Climbs peaks in Khumbu, near Mount Everest
1953	Reaches summit of Mount Everest with Tenzing Norgay on May 29; is knighted by Queen Elizabeth II; marries Louise Rose in Auckland
1954	Son Peter is born; attempts to climb Mount Makalu; receives the Hubbard Medal, the National Geographic Society's award for distinction in exploration, discovery, and research
1956	Daughter Sarah is born; departs New Zealand for Antarctica as part of the British Commonwealth Trans-Antarctic Expedition
1958	Reaches the South Pole on January 4
1959	Daughter Belinda is born
1960-61	Undertakes search for the yeti; establishes the Silver Hut on Ama Dablam; first Sherpa school is completed
1964	Lukla airstrip is built
1966	Family trip to Khumbu with Louise and the children; first Sherpa hospital is completed at Kunde
1975	Hillary moves his family from New Zealand to Nepal; Louise and Belinda are killed in a plane crash near Kathmandu
1976	Sagarmatha (Mount Everest) National Park is established
1977	"Ocean To Sky" father-son jet boat expedition up India's Ganges River
1985–89	Serves as New Zealand's High Commissioner to India, Nepal, and Bhutan
1986	Attends Tenzing Norgay's funeral in Darjeeling, India
1989	Marries June Mulgrew
1990	Son Peter climbs Mount Everest
1995	Awarded the Order of the Garter by Queen Elizabeth II
1998	Honored by the Dalai Lama for his years of service to the Tibetan people

Resource Guide

Sir Edmund Hillary's quotes are from *Nothing Venture, Nothing Win, Two Generations,* and *View from the Summit,* cited below.

Coburn, Broughton. *Everest: Mountain Without Mercy.* Washington, D.C.: National Geographic Books, 1997.

Hillary, Sir Edmund. *From the Ocean to the Sky.* London: Hodder and Stoughton, 1979.

_____. *High Adventure.* London: Hodder and Stoughton, 1955.

_____. *Nothing Venture, Nothing Win.* New York: Coward, McCann & Geoghegan, Inc., 1975.

_____. *Schoolhouse in the Clouds.* Garden City, New York: Doubleday, 1964.

_____. *View from the Summit.* London: Doubleday, 1999.

Hillary, Sir Edmund, and Desmond Doig. *High in the Thin Cold Air.* Garden City, New York: Doubleday, 1986.

Hillary, Sir Edmund, and Peter Hillary. *Two Generations.* London: Hodder and Stoughton, 1984.

Hunt, Sir John, with Sir Edmund Hillary. *The Conquest of Everest.* New York: E.P. Dutton & Company, 1954.

Stewart, Whitney, and Anne B. Keiser. *Sir Edmund Hillary: To Everest and Beyond.* Minneapolis: Lerner Publications, 1996.

Return to Everest, written and produced for National Geographic Television by Theodore Strauss.

The following articles by or about Sir Edmund Hillary have appeared in issues of NATIONAL GEOGRAPHIC:

Bishop, Barry C. 1962. "Wintering on the Roof of the World." Vol. 122, No. 4: 503–547.

Fuchs, Sir Vivian. 1959. "The Crossing of Antarctica." Vol. 115, No. 1: 25-47.

Hillary, Sir Edmund. 1955. "Beyond Everest." Vol. 108, No. 5: 579–610.

_____. 1954. "The Conquest of the Summit." Vol. 106, No. 1: 45–63.

_____. 1982. "Preserving a Mountain Heritage." Vol. 161, No. 6: 696–702.

_____. 1962. "We Build a School for Sherpa Children." Vol. 122, No. 4: 548–551.

Hunt, Brigadier Sir John. 1954. "Siege and Assault." Vol. 106, No. 1: 1–43.

Ridgeway, Rick. 1982. "Park at the Top of the World." Vol. 161, No. 6: 704–725.

Recommended Web sites:

www.mteverest.com

American Himalayan Foundation: www.bena.com/nepaltrek/ahf.html

Himalayan Explorers Club: www.hec.org

Ang Rita Sherpa, who graduated in 1971 from the first Hillary school, is now the Chief Administrator of the Himalayan Trust in Nepal.

President Eisenhower shakes Hillary's hand after presenting the Society's Hubbard Medal to the British Everest Expedition team.

In 1998 the Dalai Lama (above, right), religious leader of Tibetan Buddhists, honored Hillary for his many years of helping Sherpas in Nepal.

Index

Photographs are indicated by **boldface.** If photographs are included within a page span, the entire span is boldface.

Altitude
    effect on human body 4, 26, 29–30, 33, 42, 45, 46, 55
Ama Dablam (peak), Nepal 45, 57
Antarctica
    crossing of **38–42**
    map 38
Ayres, Harry 12, 15

Cook, Mount, New Zealand 11, 12, **12–13**

Elizabeth II, Queen (England) 35, 36, 59
Everest, Mount, China-Nepal **2–3, 20**
    Advance Base Camp (ABC) 29, **31**, 35
    Base Camp 26, 29
    British expeditions **15–36, 56**, 57
    deaths on 17, 26
    Hillary Step (rock feature) 33, 57
    map 27
    summit **32**

Fuchs, Vivian 38, 42

Hillary, Belinda 42, **43**, 51, 52, 59
Hillary, Edmund
    appointed High Commissioner 57
    climbing Mount Everest 1, **15–36, 56**, 57
    climbing Mount Makalu 45, 48
    crossing Antarctica **38–42**
    early life 8–9, **9, 10**, 11, **14**, 15
    grandmother 8, **8**, 9
    helping Sherpas **6**, 7, **45–61**
    in World War II 15
    receiving honors and awards 35, **35**, 36, 59, **63**
    studying altitude **5**
    wedding 36, **37**
    with children **43**, 59
Hillary, Gertrude Clark 8, **10**, 11
Hillary, June (sister) 9, **10**, 11
Hillary, June (wife) **60**, 61
Hillary, Louise 21, 42, **43**, 45
    death 52, 59
    wedding 36, **37**
Hillary, Peter 42, **43**, 51, 52, 57, **58–59**, 59
Hillary, Rex 9, **10**, 11, 52, 61
Hillary, Sarah 42, **43**, 51, 52
Hilllary, Percival 8–9, **10**, 11
Himalaya, Asia **2–3**, 7, 15
Himalayan Trust 51, 52, 59, 61
Hunt, John 21, 23, 24, **24**, 29, 30, **35**, 36

Kathmandu, Nepal 24, 35–36, 47, 55
Khumbu (region), Nepal 7, 24, 47, 46, 51, 55

Khumbu Icefall, Nepal 17, 18, **22–23**, 23, 29
Khumjung, Nepal
    anniversary of Everest summit **58–59**, 59
    first Sherpa school 7, 45, **46–47**, 47, 48

Lowe, George 15, **16–17**, 17, 21, **25**, 30, 33, 35, **37**

Makalu, Mount, Nepal 45, 46
Mallory, George Leigh 11, 17
Mount Everest, China-Nepal
    see Everest, Mount, China-Nepal
Mulgrew, June 45, 57
    see also Hillary, June (wife)
Mulgrew, Peter 45, 48, 61

Nepal
    airstrips built 45, 51
    destruction of forests **54**, 55
    medical care 51, **51**, 52
    mountain climbing 17
    prayer stones 52, **53**
    schools and schoolchildren **6**, 7, 45, 46, **48–49, 50**, 51, 61
New Zealand
    expedition to Antarctica **38–42**
    Hillary's wedding 36, **37**
    mountain climbing 11, 12, **12–13**, 15
Norbu, Mingma 7, 55, **55**
Norgay, Tenzing
    climbing Mount Everest 1, **21–36, 56**, 57
    death 57
    receiving honors and awards 36

Oxygen
    used to climb Mount Everest 30, **31**, 33

Sagarmatha National Park, Nepal 7, 55
Shackleton, Ernest 11, 38
Sherpas
    as climbing guides 24, **28**
    conservation efforts 7, 55, 61
    medical care 51, **51**, 52
    religious beliefs 33, 52, 57
    schools and schoolchildren **6**, 7, 45, 46, **48–49, 50**, 51, 61
    village **44**, 45
Shipton, Eric 15, 17, **18**, 21
Silver Hut (prefabricated shelter) 4, **5**, 45
South Col, Mount Everest 29–30, 33

Tengboche Lama 26, 48
Tibetan refugees 45

Yaks 24, 46, **47**
Yeti (Abominable Snowman) 26, 42, 45, footprint thought to be from 45, **45**

The world's largest nonprofit scientific and educational organization, the National Geographic Society was found-ed in 1888 "for the increase and diffusion of geographic knowledge." Since then it has supported scientific exploration and spread information to its more than nine million members worldwide.

Fulfilling this mission, the Society educates and inspires millions every day through magazines, books, television programs, videos, maps and atlases, research grants, the National Geographic Bee, teacher work-shops, and innovative classroom materials.

The Society is supported through membership dues and income from the sale of its educational products. For more information about the National Geographic Society and its educational programs and publications, please call 1-800-NGS-LINE (647-5463), or visit our Web site: www.nationalgeographic.com